The Let's Talk Library™

Let's Talk About
Down Syndrome

Melanie Apel Gordon

The Rosen Publishing Group's
PowerKids Press™
New York

For Mom, Carol Apel, a very special caregiver. With love, Melanie.

Published in 1999 by The Rosen Publishing Group, Inc.
29 East 21st Street, New York, NY 10010

First Edition

Book Design: Erin McKenna

Photo Credits: Cover, p. 8 © Mimi Cotter/International Stock Photo, p. 4 © Arthur Tilley/FPG International, p. 7 © V. I. Lab E. R. I. C./FPG International, p. 11 © Laurie Bayer/International Stock Photo, p. 12 © Rob Gage/FPG International, p. 15 © Jeff Kaufman/FPG International, p.16 © Frank Grant/International Stock Photo, p. 19 © Bill Tucker/ International Stock Photo, p. 20 © Beatriz Schiller.

Gordon, Melanie Apel.
    Let's talk about down syndrome / by Melanie Apel Gordon.
        p.   cm.— (Let's talk library)
    Includes index.
    Summary: Describes what causes Down syndrome and how it affects those children who have it, stressing how they can be helped to lead happy lives.
    ISBN 0-8239-5197-9
    1. Down syndrome—Juvenile literature. [1. Down syndrome. 2. Mentally handicapped.] I. Title.
II. Series.
RJ506.D68G67 1998
618.92'858842—dc21

                                                    97-46860
                                                        CIP
                                                         AC

Manufactured in the United States of America

Table of Contents

Teddy and Casey

Teddy and Casey are brothers. They ride the school bus and play baseball together. Teddy and Casey are both in third grade, but they are not the same age. Casey is eight, and Teddy is ten. They are in the same grade because Teddy has **Down syndrome** (DOWN SIN-drohm). Because of this, Teddy is **developmentally delayed** (deh-vel-up-MEN-tuh-lee de-LAYD). Even though Teddy is older, he learns things slower than Casey does. But Casey is proud of the things Teddy can do.

◀ A child with Down syndrome can do many of the same things that a child without Down syndrome can do, such as play on a baseball team like these two boys.

What's a Chromosome?

Our bodies are made up of millions of tiny parts called **cells** (SELZ). All the cells work together to make our bodies work. A **chromosome** (KROH-muh-sohm) is a tiny part of a cell. Chromosomes contain **genes** (JEENZ). Genes tell your cells what color your hair will be, and even if you'll be a girl or boy. Chromosomes make you **unique** (yoo-NEEK). You have 23 chromosomes from your mom, and 23 from your dad. Kids who have Down syndrome have one extra chromosome.

This shows different parts of a cell. The green part is called the nucleus. This is where your chromosomes are. ▶

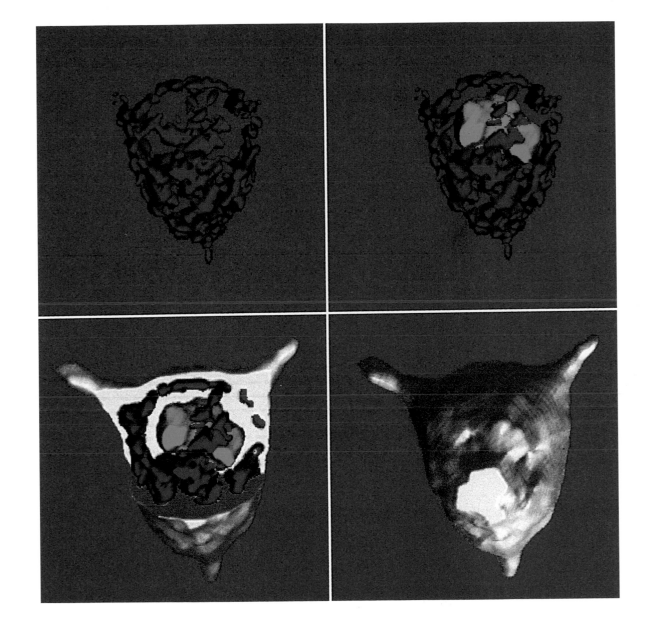

Chromosome 21

Scientists have given our chromosomes numbers. People who have Down syndrome have an extra number 21 chromosome. This extra chromosome causes trouble. Kids who have Down syndrome look different from other kids. Their eyes may slant up a little bit, their noses are usually small, and they often have wide hands and short fingers. Most kids with Down syndrome are smaller than other kids their age. But even though they may look and act differently, they are kids, just like you.

◀ This little girl has Down syndrome.

Who Has Down Syndrome?

Down syndrome can't be cured or prevented. You can't catch Down syndrome from someone who has it either. Kids who have Down syndrome are born with it. Anyone can have a baby who has Down syndrome. But women who have babies after the age of 35 are more likely to give birth to a baby who has Down syndrome than younger women.

One out of every 800 babies born in the United States has Down syndrome. ▶

Testing for Down Syndrome

Before a baby is born, doctors can do a test to see if the baby will have Down syndrome. The doctor will take a sample of the baby's cells and look for the extra number 21 chromosome. If the doctor finds it, the baby will have Down syndrome. Parents may choose to have this test so they will know all the facts before their baby is born.

◀ Many parents like to know if their unborn baby has Down syndrome.

Heart Trouble

The extra number 21 chromosome is a real troublemaker. About half of the kids who have Down syndrome have problems with their hearts. Doctors check all babies born with Down syndrome to see if they have heart problems. Most of the time the doctors can fix the babies' hearts. Kids with Down syndrome may have other health problems too. But doctors can heal many of these problems. Kids who have Down syndrome can live long and healthy lives.

The doctor listens to this girl's heart just the way he listens to the heart of a child with Down syndrome. ▶

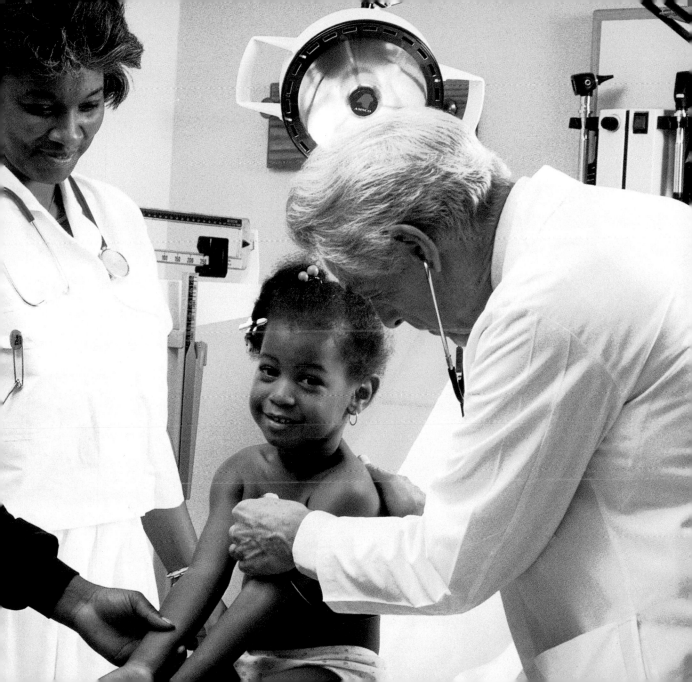

Getting a Head Start

Kids who have Down syndrome learn more slowly than other kids do. Babies with Down syndrome can get a head start on learning by going to a special school when they are just a few months old. Here they get extra help from **physical therapists** (FIH-zih-kul THER-uh-pists), **occupational therapists** (ahk-yoo-PAY-shun-ul THER-uh-pists), and **speech therapists** (SPEECH THER-uh-pists). These people help the babies learn to sit up, crawl, play, and talk. The therapists are very important people.

◀ There are all kinds of physical therapy. This girl is strengthening her legs with exercises in a pool.

At School

Some kids who have Down syndrome go to special schools. Others go to regular schools. No matter what school they go to, they learn reading, writing, and math. When they get older they may go to high school. Some kids who have Down syndrome may stay in high school until they are 21 years old. After high school many kids with Down syndrome get jobs.

A student in your class may have Down syndrome. ▶

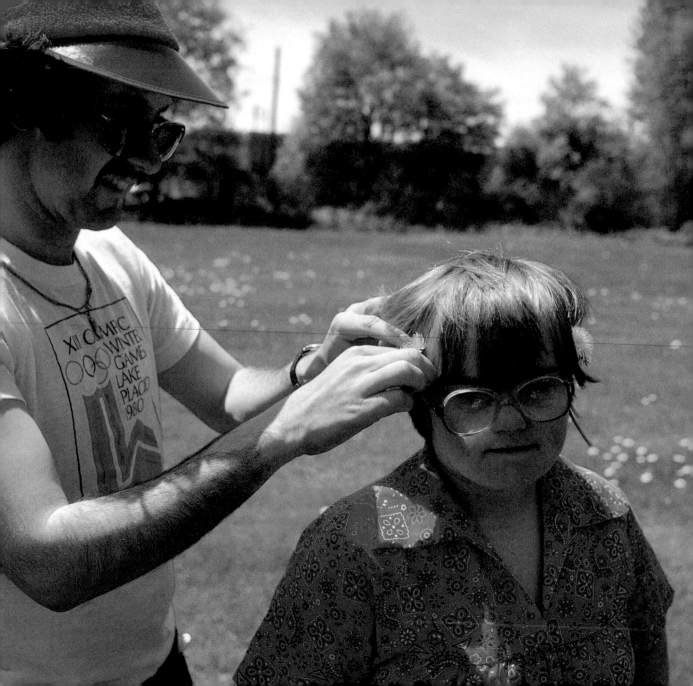

Growing Up

Helping around the house, going to the movies, and spending time with friends are many things that kids with Down syndrome like to do. Most kids who have Down syndrome work hard to learn everyday skills so that one day they might be **independent** (in-de-PEN-dent). Down syndrome doesn't go away. But with lots of love and care, kids who have Down syndrome grow up to be happy, healthy adults.

◀ Playing with friends and spending time outside are things that all kids like to do.

Just Like Other Kids

Kids who have Down syndrome are very much like other kids. They like to do the same things that you do. They like to watch TV, play sports, and read. It just might take a kid with Down syndrome a little bit longer to learn how to do the things that you can do. People with Down syndrome may be a little different. But they are still fun and loving people.

Glossary

cell (SEL) One of many tiny units that make up the human body.

chromosome (KROH-muh-sohm) The part of cells that hold the genes.

developmentally delayed (deh-vel-up-MEN-tuh-lee de-LAYD) When someone learns things more slowly than other people do.

Down syndrome (DOWN SIN-drohm) A condition caused by an extra chromosome.

gene (JEEN) A part of a chromosome; a gene tells your cells what your body will be like.

independent (in-de-PEN-dent) Thinking for or taking care of oneself.

occupational therapist (ahk-yoo-PAY-shun-ul THER-uh-pist) A person who helps other people use their hands to do small tasks.

physical therapist (FIH-zih-kul THER-uh-pist) A person who helps other people walk and move.

speech therapist (SPEECH THER-uh-pist) A person who helps other people learn to speak better.

unique (yoo-NEEK) One of a kind.

Index